MONKEYS & APES

An animal fact book

Written by Alfred Brockman

Photographs by Philip Craven *F.M.P.A.*

Library of Congress Cataloging in Publication Data

Brockman, Alfred.
  Monkeys & apes.

  (An Animal fact book)
  Summary: Brief text and photographs introduce the physical characteristics, habits, and natural environment of monkeys and apes.
  1. Monkeys—Juvenile literature.   2. Apes—Juvenile literature.   [1. Monkeys.   2. Apes] I. Craven, Philip, ill.   II. Title.   III. Title: Monkeys and apes.
QL737.P9B766   1986   599.8'2   85-28985
ISBN 0-86592-922-X

Monkeys and apes are our closest relatives in the animal world.

They are known as "primates," which means "first." They are very smart animals.

Most have five fingers or toes on each limb.

This mother with her child is a gibbon, the smallest of the apes.

Most monkeys and apes are found in countries where the weather is warm.

Except for the baboons, which prefer the ground, monkeys live in trees. They have great skill in moving through the branches.

This squirrel monkey comes from South America.

Unlike apes that have hardly any tails, monkeys have long, strong tails. They put these to good use when climbing trees.

The gorilla from Africa has a roar. The chimpanzee gives a gruff bark. The howls of the gibbon can be heard a mile away. The smaller monkeys make a whistling noise.

Most apes and monkeys, like these chimpanzees, live in families or groups. They hunt and feed together.

They will join together to fight any outsider who may want to take over their home ground.

Monkeys usually use all their limbs to walk. The leaders, however, walk upright like a man.

All monkeys have very good eyesight.
Their eyes are large.

Their hearing is also very good.
However, they cannot smell very well.

Monkeys like to eat fruits and
vegetables.

Apes are larger than monkeys. The gorilla is the largest.

An adult gorilla can weigh as much as 600 pounds.

They are peaceful animals, and they rarely attack unless they have to defend themselves.

This is a macaque monkey which is partly related to the African baboon.

There are many kinds of monkeys. Some have longer tails than others.

The macaque monkeys from East India have tails nearly as long as their heads and bodies.

Spider monkeys can pick up objects with their tails.

The Hamadryas baboons were great favorites of the Egyptians in the olden days.

They are known as "dog faced" monkeys.

When they see enemies coming, they throw stones at them.

The baboon will stop its young one from straying by holding it by the tail.

Next to the gorilla, the orangutan is the largest ape.

Orangutans can weigh as much as 200 pounds. They are about four feet tall.

Their arm spread will reach almost eight feet.

Orangutans have shaggy hair. When they swing through the trees they can move faster than a man running on the ground.

At night they build sleeping shelves in the trees.

In winter, when they make their beds, they cover themselves with blankets of leaves.

The mandrill is the largest baboon from West Africa.

You can tell the one in the picture is a male by its unusual face markings. The nose is red while the ridges on the face are blue.

They make a colorful sight when walking in the forests.